# ESCAPE ROOM PUZZLES
# DINOSAUR ISLAND

**KINGFISHER**
LONDON & NEW YORK

Copyright © Macmillan Publishers
International Ltd 2022
First published in 2022 by Kingfisher,
120 Broadway, New York, NY 10271
Kingfisher is an imprint of Macmillan
Children's Books, London
All rights reserved.

Distributed in the U.S. and Canada
by Macmillan, 120 Broadway,
New York, NY 10271

Library of Congress
Cataloging-in-Publication
data has been applied for.

Designed, edited, and project
managed by Dynamo Limited.

ISBN: 978-0-7534-7682-6

Kingfisher books are available for
special promotions and premiums.
For details contact: Special Markets
Department, Macmillan, 120 Broadway,
New York, NY 10271.

For more information, please visit
www.kingfisherbooks.com

Printed in China
9 8 7 6 5 4 3 2 1
1TR/1221/RV/WKT/120WF

# ESCAPE ROOM PUZZLES
# DINOSAUR ISLAND

KINGFISHER
LONDON & NEW YORK

# CONTENTS

# MEET THE TEAM!

Hey! I'm Kiran.

Ethan here!

**NAME:** Kiran

**STRENGTHS:** Leader and organizer

**FUN FACT:** Loves extreme sports–especially rock climbing

**NAME:** Ethan

**STRENGTHS:** Math and science genius

**FUN FACT:** Amazing memory for facts and always wins any quiz

Hello! Zane's the name.

Hi!

**NAME:** Zane

**STRENGTHS:** Creative and thinks outside the box

**FUN FACT:** Loves art and takes his trusty sketchbook wherever he goes

**NAME:** Cassia

**STRENGTHS:** Technology pro

**FUN FACT:** Queen of gadgets and invents her own apps

# WELCOME!

**Kiran, Ethan, Zane, and Cassia are on a mission and they need YOUR help!**

Zane's grandmother, Zinnia, worked at the dinosaur museum long ago and she told Zane about a piece of missing dinosaur research that needs returning to the exhibition! Zinnia remembers the museum has a secret route to a mysterious underground island filled with real-life dinosaurs and top-secret labs where they carried out research. Fortunately, today Zane and his friends are on a school trip to the museum.

## YOUR MISSION:

Crack codes, solve sequences, and master mazes to help the friends complete their mission and make it back before anyone notices they're missing. Ready, set . . . puzzle!

## WHAT YOU KNOW:

- There is a vault under the museum that leads to a secret island.

- Zane's grandmother has given him a scrap of paper with a symbol on it. What could it mean?

- She also gave Zane this riddle, which will come in handy in Room One.

Mysterious symbol

### Important!

In each of the five rooms, there will be a number that you must collect. Don't forget to jot these down as you go along. You'll need them to successfully complete the mission.

### Riddle!

I have buttons but I am not a cardigan.

I have doors but you don't need a key.

I take you up and down while you stand still.

What am I?

# ROOM ONE:
# THE STEGOSAURUS ROOM

Welcome to the museum! Your school trip starts here, which means that it's time to start your special mission. After weeks of planning, everyone is super excited to finally be at the museum. You have the clues from Zane's grandmother and a whole museum to navigate. But the question is, can you complete the mission before your teacher notices that you're missing?

While your classmates are listening to a talk on dinosaurs, you all decide to hang back a bit. This seems like a good time to begin searching for clues. Zane is focused on sketching everything he sees, and Ethan has found a guidebook. Meanwhile, Cassia and Kiran lead the way and tell the others to follow them into the **Stegosaurus Room**. What challenges will be waiting inside?

There will be some magnificent model dinosaurs and skeletons to discover in this room. Keep a note of anything you see that might come in handy later on!

# SPOT THE DINO DIFFERENCES

While the group of friends begin to explore the Stegosaurus Room, Zane goes quiet. He's noticed that something's not right. Take a look at the picture below and see if you can find the 10 differences between the guidebook and the room. Circle each change you identify!

Come and explore the . . .
**Stegosaurus Room**

5

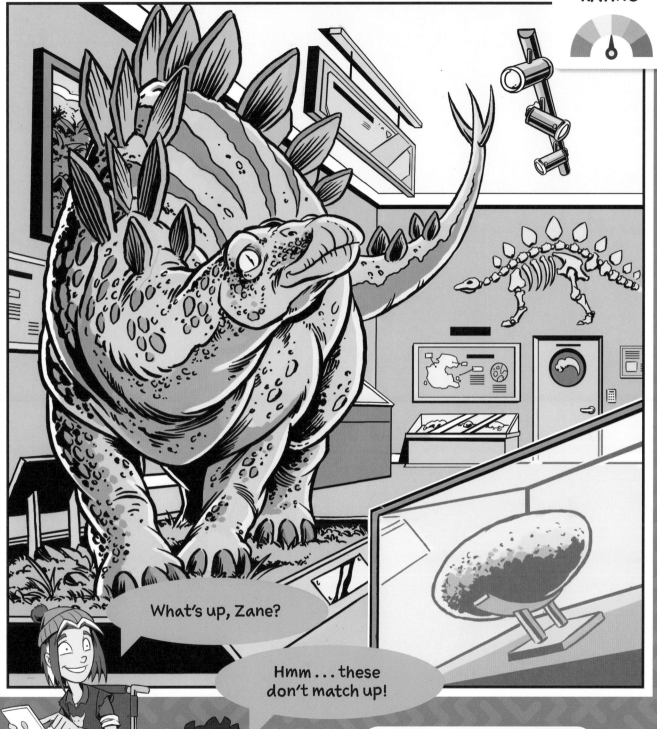

## DINO FACT

The name *Stegosaurus* means "roofed lizard," referring to the triangular plates along the dinosaur's back. These beasts were big enough for a roof, too—*Stegosaurus* could reach as long as 30 feet (9 meters).

# LAST CHANCE

The friends closely examine all the things that have changed. Ethan finds what looks like the doors to an elavator with a keycode panel next to it. The doors are firmly closed, and after a couple of attempts to open them a red light starts flashing and the display reads "LAST CHANCE." Just then, Cassia notices a scrap of paper tucked behind one of the museum display cases . . .

Aha! The answer to Zinnia's riddle was an ELAVATOR.

So you know what that means, right? Yep, we've got to find a way to unlock these doors and get to another floor. We need you to reveal the code!

Grab a pencil to connect up the prime numbers in each square from smallest to biggest.

Can you find the hidden number inside each square?

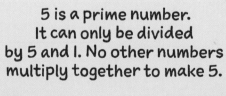

5 is a prime number. It can only be divided by 5 and 1. No other numbers multiply together to make 5.

## What's a prime number?

A prime number can only be divided by 1 or by itself.

The PRIME thing to remember if you want to GO DOWN to the lab is to JOIN numbers in order!

**1**

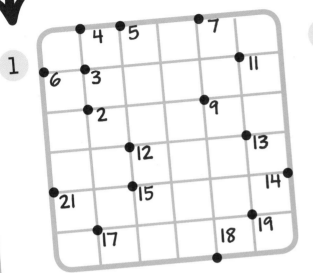

**2**

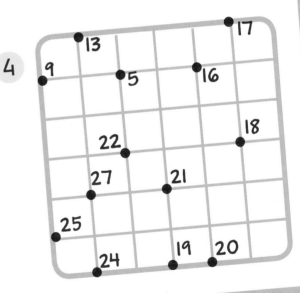

**3**

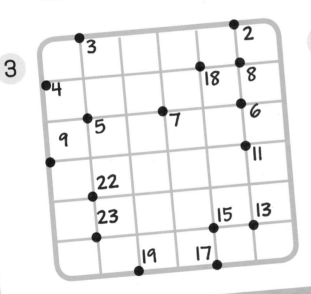

**4**

Write your code here:

Nice work! Come on, everyone in the elavator.

# TOPSY TURVY

Well done! The code you typed in granted access to the elavator. As you get in, you find the buttons to make the elavator move are locked by a peculiar panel. It doesn't take long before Kiran realizes that you need to rearrange the tiles on the panel.

Fill in the numbers so you know the right order to press the tiles, from top left to bottom right.

Copy the designs from the grid on page 14 into the correct squares.

We need to put the logo from the guidebook back together in here.

## 🦖 DINO FACT

Sharing an elavator with a dinosaur wouldn't be ideal! But if you had to, a *Lesothosaurus* would be a good choice. These herbivores (plant eaters) were only about the size of a large chicken—meaning there would be plenty of room to share in that elevator, plus they wouldn't want to eat you!

## Yikes!

The elavator takes you to an abandoned floor—it's a secret passageway. You check the guidebook, but this floor has been crossed out on the map so you can't read it. Cassia scans it with her app and it reveals the words "Vault X" . . .

# ROOM TWO:
# VAULT X

Awesome job, team! You have successfully escaped from the first room and now you find yourself in a passageway. Each of the narrow corridors leads to—you guessed it—more corridors and more doors!

Zane has his trusty sketchbook at the ready to help keep track of all the clues you've seen so far. Cassia's handy app has made the crossed-out map visible again and has helped her figure out that **Vault X** is around here somewhere. The only problem is, you will need to find your way through the labyrinth of tangled paths first.

And just in case all of this wasn't tricky enough, these corridors are also rigged with a complex alarm system, so watch out! The last thing that you want is to be caught before you've completed your mission.

# LIGHTS OUT

You take a turn down one of the corridors when suddenly all the lights go out. If you're going to reach Vault X, you have to make it through this mirror maze to turn on the power switch. Luckily, everyone has brought flashlights with them, but whose flashlight will lead to the switch? Read page 19 for the instructions.

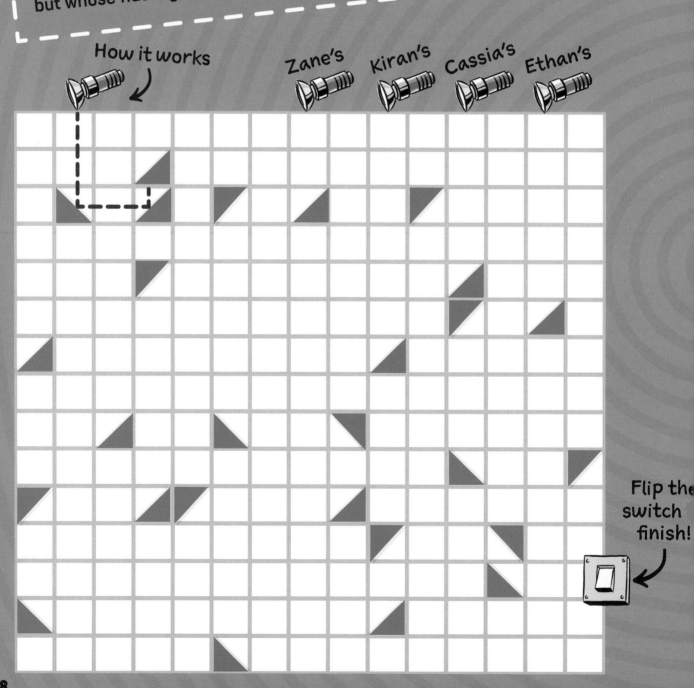

How it works

Zane's   Kiran's   Cassia's   Ethan's

Flip the switch finish!

Which flashlight leads to the power switch? To start, draw a straight line from a flashlight until you reach a mirror. When your flashlight's beam hits the mirror, you must change direction and draw a line until you reach the next mirror. Keep going like that until you reach the finish.

🐾 You can only change direction when you land on a mirror.

🐾 You can move in straight lines that go up and down or side to side, but not diagonally.

The back of the mirror means you've hit a dead end so you'll need to start again.

Landing on this side of the mirror means you can change direction.

 **DINO FACT**

Did you know that some dinosaurs had night vision? The lights going out would be no problem if you were a *Velociraptor*! These carnivores (meat eaters) had excellent night vision and could hunt for prey at night.

## Awesome!

You made it! Let's see where this corridor takes us.

# DUPLICATE DINOS

At the end of the maze, Kiran finds a deck of jumbled-up cards! Maybe one of these cards holds a clue for where to go next? Your task is to find the odd one out. Draw lines to match up, or cross out, all of the pairs until there is only one left.

You have found the odd one out. You turn it over and find this clue. Will it show you which way to go next?

From afar I may look like a bubbling cauldron.

Dare to look a little closer, and you will hear my roar.

## Good work!

You keep the card and explore the passageway. You find a cobweb-covered door with a symbol over it—it's the one that Zane's grandmother told him about. It's also the symbol that the clue was describing, so this must be the right way!

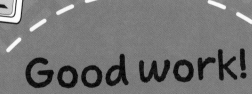

# CHAIN REACTION

As you move into the next room, you enter a passage with eight doors. You need to unlock each one in the correct order to deactivate the alarms before opening the final door that leads to Vault X. Can you work out the correct order using the clues below and on page 23?

Door ____

Door 4

Door ____

Door 2

Door ____

Door 7

Door ____

Door 6

## Clues

1. The third door to be unlocked is 2.

2. The green door must be unlocked directly before door 2.

3. The final door has a primary color.

4. Door 7 must be unlocked immediately before 5.

5. The fifth door to be unlocked is pink.

6. Door 6 should be unlocked just before door 1.

7. Unlock door 8 first.

8. Between door 1 and door 7, unlock number 4.

These doors are numbered illogically!

____ ____ ____ ____

Write the numbers in order here!

## Clues

Door 1 - mix white and red to get this color.

Door 3 - mix blue and yellow to get this color.

Door 5 - mix this color with red to make orange.

Door 8 - mix blue and red to make this color.

Not so fast, some of the room numbers are missing from the control panel. You need to figure out which number belongs to which door. Read the clues to help you fill in the blanks!

## Aced it!

You manage to deactivate the alarms in the correct sequence. The final door swings open and you step inside Vault X . . .

# THE VAULT

You've unlocked all of the doors in the correct order and deactivated the alarm. But now you are face to face with Vault X. Surprise, surprise—it's locked. Honestly, how much security can a secret island have? To gain access, you must swipe your finger along the buttons in the correct order. Luckily, Zane has his sketchbook, so he's drawing out a few combinations on paper to avoid setting off the alarm!

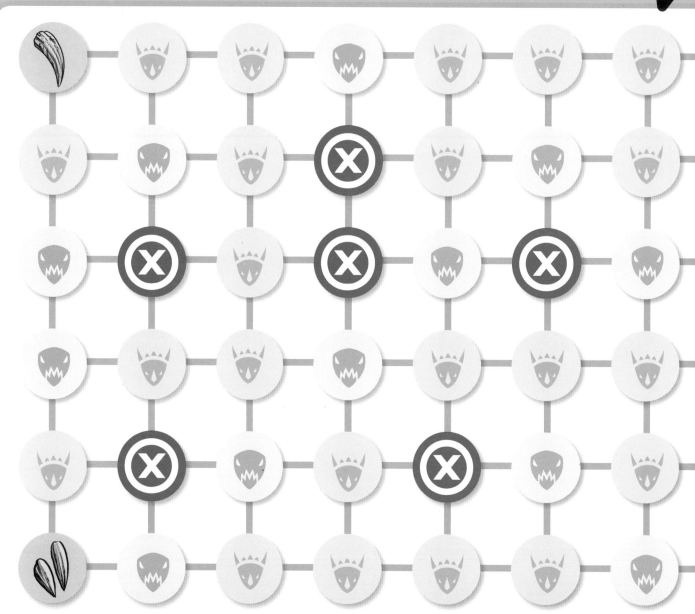

Find out which fossil you need to start on in order to reach the "ACCESS AUTHORIZED" key. Once you leave a fossil, you can't swipe over a symbol twice in a row. You are not permitted to move diagonally or on the red buttons, so be sure to follow the lines.

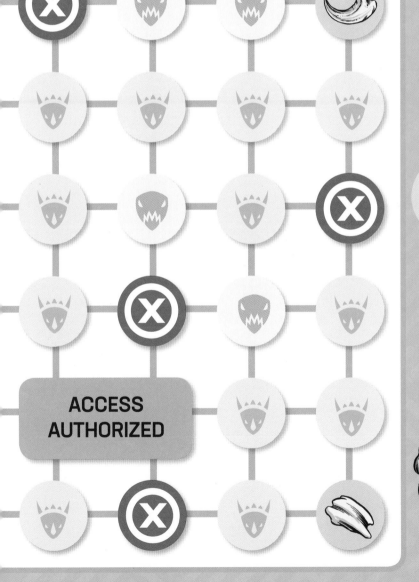

ACCESS AUTHORIZED

# At last!

The vault door swings open and a scared baby *Triceratops* appears. The team name it Toppy! Now you're going to have to find its parents as well as track down the missing research!

Looks like Toppy needs to get to Dinosaur Island as much as we do!

# ROOM THREE:
# SCIENTISTS' LAB

You've made it through the vault to the next room and that means that you are one step closer to completing your mission. The coolest part of it all is that you now have Toppy by your side—and that can only be a good thing, right? The guidebook says that this third room is a scientists' lab. It is full of tanks and test tubes containing weird and wonderful dinosaur specimens. Judging by how hard it was to get into this room, the studies going on in here must have been top secret.

Will you discover any clues that will help lead you closer to the missing research? Keep an eye out for any numbers!

# OPEN THE BOX

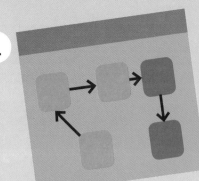

You find yourself in a totally different kind of room. The walls are lined with capsules containing what look like sleeping baby dinosaurs, suspended in strange-colored liquid. In the center of the room is a huge mechanical crate that must have once held a dinosaur—maybe it holds a clue for the team now? You peer inside but it's too dark to see anything. On the outside you spot an electronic access keypad—but what's the entry code? There are five pink notes scattered all around, and they all have different codes written on them.

Only one note can gain you access to the crate—the others will get the team locked out! Can you identify which note is the one to follow so you can open the crate and see what's inside?

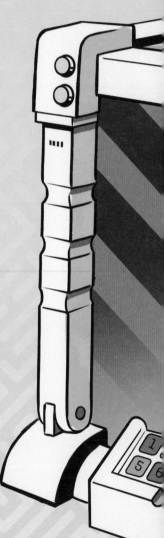

## Hint

Test the instructions on each note before you enter the code!

Zane remembers his grandmother telling him about a five-digit security code where **no number is repeated**. It looks like you need to type the code in here.

The last number is six times the first number. The second number is half the third. The fourth number is 6.

**3**

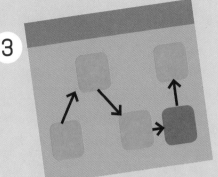

**4**

The second digit and the fourth digit add up to 8. The first and the third digit add up to 16.

**5**

The five digits add up to 38.

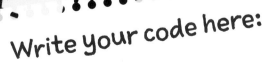

Write your code here:

___ ___ ___ ___ ___

# Epic!

You enter the code and the crate opens up. All that's in there is another note telling you to look at the computer terminal for more answers . . .

# STEP CAREFULLY

Here's the sequence

Ethan finds a computer terminal in the corner of the room—maybe it holds a clue to where the missing research is, or how to get Toppy back home? The screen is covered with colorful symbols. Across the top, it reads: "**Use the touchscreen to unlock the safe. Follow the sequence on the right. Remember you can move up, down, left and right, but NOT diagonally.**" Alongside the words there are five symbols. Can you find your way from top left to bottom right?

Start here

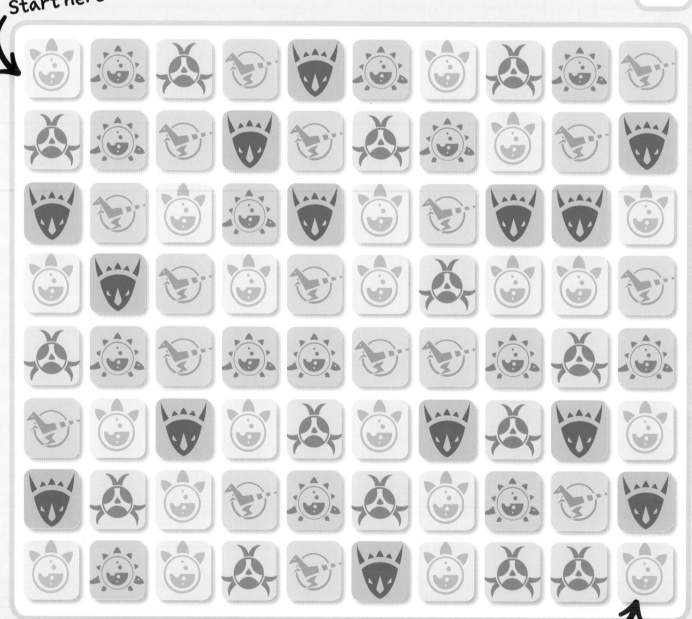

You made it!

## 🦖 DINO FACT

Dinosaur footprints found preserved in rock are called ichnites. They are often found in what would have been soft mud, which was baked by the Sun over many days or even months. Paleontologists examine each one closely to figure out exactly which dinosaur made them.

## Phew!

Across the room, the door of a large safe swings open with a crash.

# UNLOCKED

Awesome job, team! You've unlocked the safe, so what next? Cassia has found a key code stuck to the inside of the safe. She has worked out that each symbol has a value. Can you fill in the blanks to find out what each symbol is worth? Use the first two numbers to help you!

Use these numbers to unlock the door!

= 5    = 3    =___    =___    =___

Hey, look at this!

If we calculate these sums, we can fill in the blanks.

 +  =

 X  =

 −  =

## 🦖 DINO FACT

If you need a dino to help you reach the experiments hidden high up on the shelves, the sauropods are your best bet! This subgroup of dinosaurs include the largest to ever live, with long necks and long tails. They ranged from 20 feet (6 meters) to 200 feet (60 meters) long and could weigh up to 80 tons.

## Well done!

Ethan finds a door and tries the code. The lock clicks open to reveal another secret lab!

# DISTORTED DINOS

You run into the next secret lab and find lots of tanks with dinosaur specimens bobbing around inside them. Zane recognizes them from the sketches in the guidebook and concludes the team must be heading in the right direction. Following the exact specimens should lead you closer to Dinosaur Island! Can you match the guidebook pictures to the dinos in the tanks?

Guidebook pictures

Woah, check these out! Are there seriously dinosaurs in those tanks?

This is incredible. Now I need to determine which ones match the pictures in the guidebook.

1

2

3

4

Look at each row to identify which test tube dino matches the image in the book exactly. Circle the answers.

CHALLENGE RATING

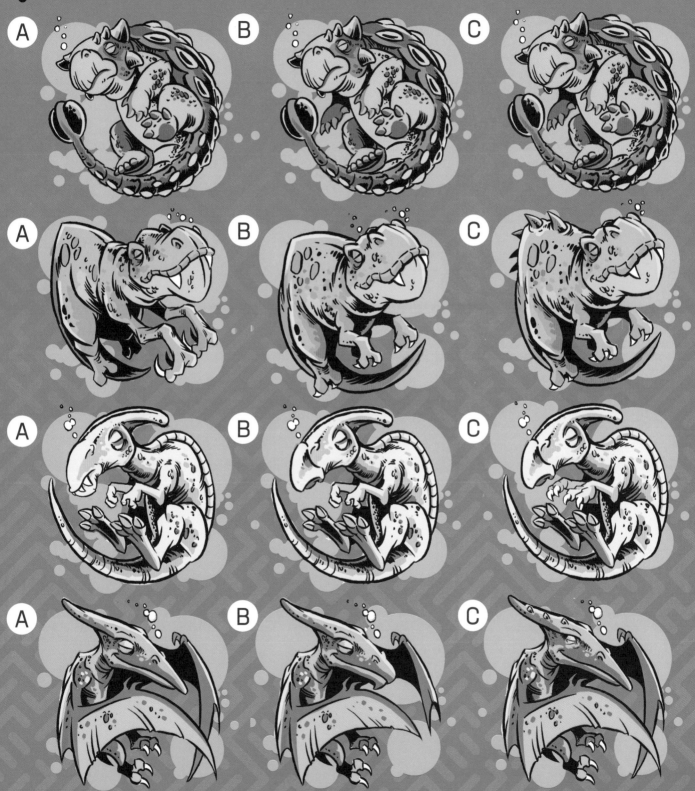

A    B    C

A    B    C

A    B    C

A    B    C

# CABLE CAPERS

Following the specimens leads you to a tiny dark store room with more tanks. If you are going to have any chance of seeing what's inside them, or anything at all in this room, you will need to turn their lights back on. But can you figure out which one turns on each tank? Two of the switches will reactivate the alarm system, so be careful.

# ROOM FOUR:
# THE FINAL LAB

You escape yet another room and race down the corridor with the research notes that you have just collected. Kiran figures out that the passcode to open the door has something to do with the numbers from the tanks in the previous room. Luckily, Zane had written them down in his sketch pad! He eagerly types them in and the door clicks open.

You are now in . . . ANOTHER lab! But don't give up yet. This lab is totally different from the last one—it has a dinosaur hatchery, feeding station, and tons of fossils. You know you are heading in the right direction because the research notes you picked up in the last room tell you to go straight to the big door ahead.

# SAFE PATH

Dodge the danger spots (red stars) as you race for the door, but don't forget to pick up the dinosaur food (green circle) and the door password (yellow circle) on your way. You can't back-track or cross your own path, so can you find the best route through the dinosaur hatchery?

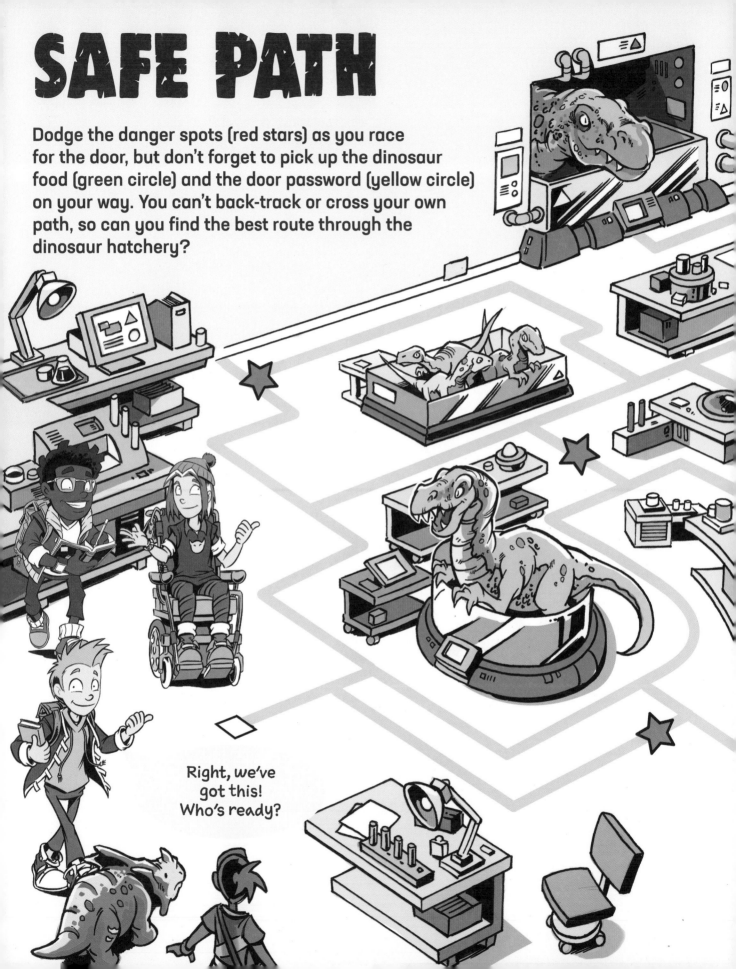

Right, we've got this! Who's ready?

 **DINO FACT**

You may be guiding a baby dinosaur through the lab, but it would be far harder for a fully-grown *Triceratops* to get through the door—its skull could grow up to 8 feet (2.4 meters) long!

# Nice footwork!

But don't even think about stopping for a rest! Time to enter the next room.

# CODE CRACKER

Phew! You managed to avoid all those hungry dinosaurs, but now you have a whole new challenge—how to get through the sealed door at the end of the lab. Luckily, you were smart enough to grab the door password from the desk . . . but can you figure out the correct order to press the buttons to release the lock?

## Attention researchers:

After the recent break-ins, all door locks have been reset and new passcodes have been assigned. To open the door, use the following clues to figure out the combination of buttons to press. After three attempts you will be locked out—good luck!

- Whatever you do, don't press red first.
- The last two buttons both have more than three sides.
- Make sure the final button is a color that can be mixed with another color to make purple.

## Ha! Ha! Ha!

What do you call a dinosaur that never gives up?

Try-Try-Try-ceratops!

Try out your answers here!

ATTEMPT 1

ATTEMPT 2

Third time's the charm!

ATTEMPT 3

OK, here it goes!

## 🦖 DINO FACT

If you needed to pick a smart dinosaur to help you out with these tricky challenges, a *Troodon* would've been a good call. *Troodon*'s brain was pretty big compared to its size. It also had excellent vision thanks to its big, beady, forward-facing eyes.

# Nice work!

The door clicks open and you're through. But what will you face in the next room?

# FOSSIL FRENZY

You enter a room filled with shelf after shelf of fossils. Kiran remembers seeing something about fossils in the research notes picked up in the room of tanks. But when she finds it, the page is ripped. Can you put it back together?

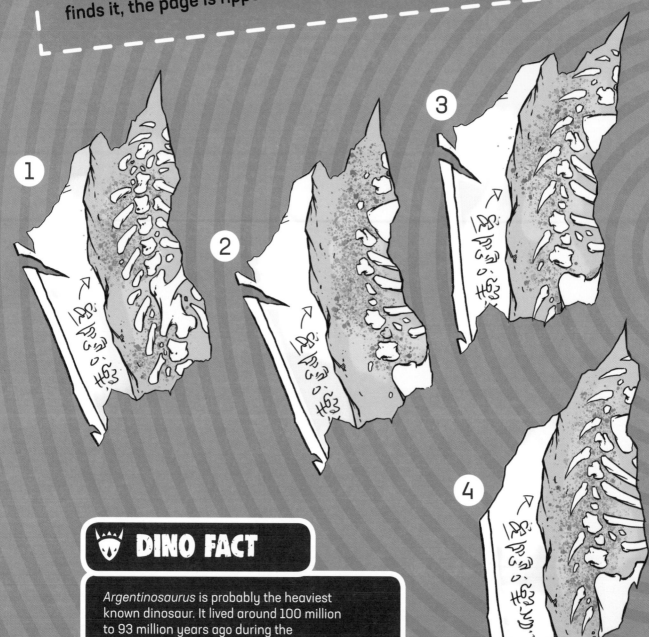

## 🐲 DINO FACT

*Argentinosaurus* is probably the heaviest known dinosaur. It lived around 100 million to 93 million years ago during the Cretaceous period. It is estimated that it weighed between 77 and 110 tons.

# Keep digging!

On the reverse of the page is a handwritten note which says "*Giganotosaurus* fossils, location: Dinosaur Island." Could this be part of the missing research they must retrieve from Dinosaur Island and bring back to the museum? Better keep digging!

# FOSSIL HUNTING

You're excitedly studying the bones when you come across a mysterious rolled-up scroll. It's covered with different sequences of fossils. Then Cassia has an idea! She uses her app to scan the room and in the far corner finds a keypad with the same symbols as on the scroll. It looks like you need to find all six combinations in the grid.

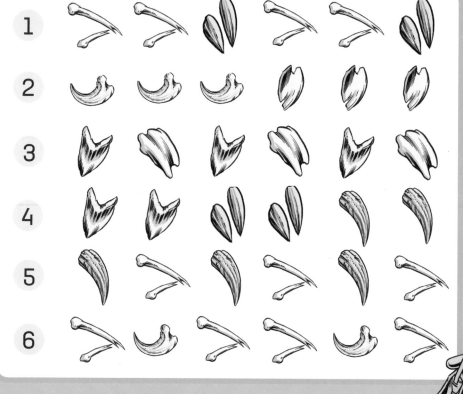

I have an idea . . .

## Ha! Ha! Ha!

What do you call a fossil
that does nothing all day?
Lazy bones!

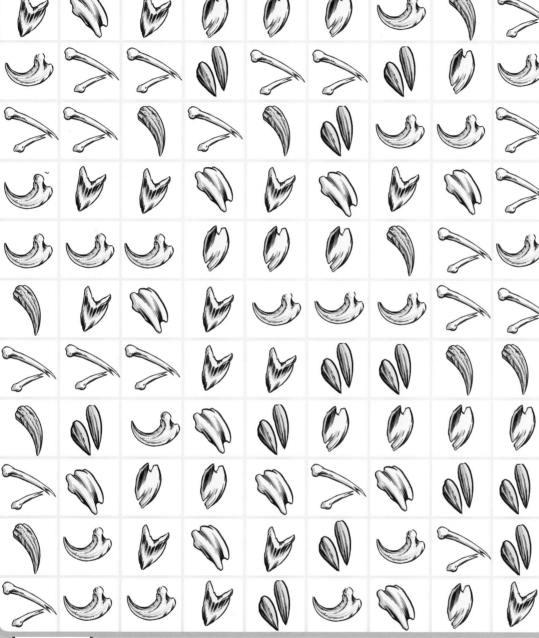

**4**

**DINO FACT**

Some fossils are so small they can only be seen using a microscope! They're called microfossils.

# Wow!

Cassia types in the sequences and a message appears on the screen: "Access to Dinosaur Island granted. Select the star key to be transported." Cassia presses the star key and . . .

# ROOM FIVE:
# DINOSAUR ISLAND

Your hard work has paid off! You find yourselves transported to a strange landscape full of plants you've never seen before. Could this be the mysterious island Zane's grandmother talked about?

As your eyes adjust to the light, you notice a number of real-life dinosaurs roaming around. It looks like you might be facing your greatest challenge yet.

Cassia found an old map in the book of research notes and has scanned it into her tablet. She looks around at landmarks to locate where you are and begins to plot a route across the island. But not before she warns the others that they must be prepared to cross lakes, hop between islands, and dodge dangerous dinos.

# LAY OF THE LAND

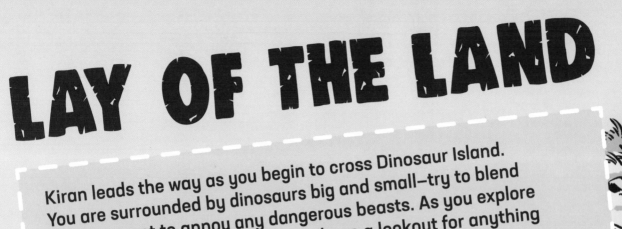

Kiran leads the way as you begin to cross Dinosaur Island. You are surrounded by dinosaurs big and small—try to blend in and try not to annoy any dangerous beasts. As you explore the island, Zane thinks it's wise to keep a lookout for anything that may have been left by researchers.

Check off each of these items when you find it hidden in the picture.

3

# X MARKS THE SPOT

Cassia has been studying the map and found the locations of a number of dig sites. It looks like dinosaurs that lived here millions of years ago have been brought back to life from their fossils. As Cassia scans her tablet, some instructions appear on screen that could lead to the dig site. Can you follow the instructions and find the right spot?

My app is telling us something.

**Follow the instructions and add an "X" in the square you land on.**

**Step 1:** Travel 5 squares east past the volcano.

**Step 2:** Move 2 squares south east toward the coast.

**Step 3:** Now go west 3 squares and south 1 square. Avoid the forest—it's full of carnivores!

**Step 4:** Hug the edge of the lake and travel south west 1 square.

**Step 5:** Move 3 squares west and 1 square north.

Check your directions with this compass!

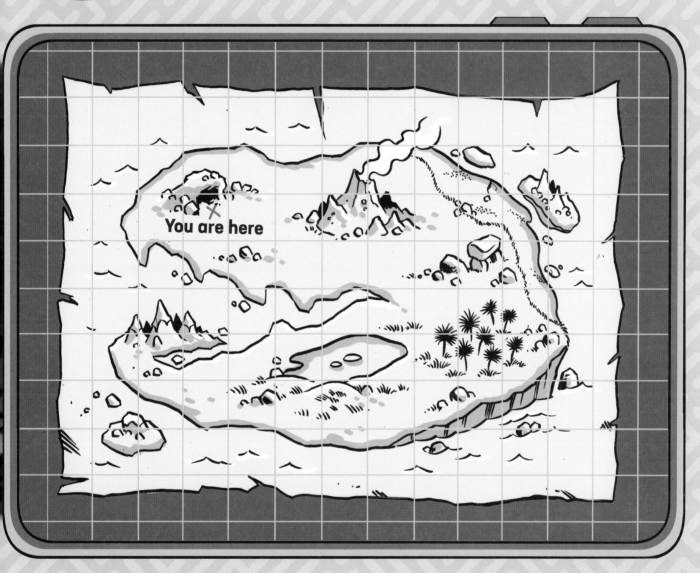
You are here

## 🦖 DINO FACT

*Ornithomimosauria* (or ostrich mimics) were a species of dinosaur from the Mesozoic era. They could run at speeds of 25 miles (40 kilometers) per hour or faster! The species had long limbs that made them look ostrich-like, which is how they got their name.

## Made it!

Everyone starts hunting around for evidence of the dig site. Turn the page to see what you find.

# UNCOVER THE TRUTH

They planted dummy capsules to throw us off the scent!

You get to the spot marked on the map. Surrounding the team are various mounds of disturbed earth. Buried in each one is a capsule marked with the same symbol that is on the piece of paper Zane's grandmother gave him. This must be the missing research! Zane flips over the paper from his grandmother and on the back is a clue that might help everyone figure out which capsule is the right one to open.

This is the correct capsule. Do you think you can find it by looking at the images on page 55?

# TOOTHY T-REX

Oh no! On your way back, you forget to avoid the forest and run straight into a grumpy *T-rex*. Three of her teeth are missing and she wants them back before she will even think about letting anyone past. Can you figure out which ones they are?

# ALMOST!

Phew, you make it past the *T-rex* alive, but it's not over yet! You find a family of *Triceratops* inside a compound. You must complete each grid to unlock the gate and reunite Toppy with its family.

This one has already been done!

1

## Ha! Ha! Ha!

What dinosaur could jump higher than a house?
All of them! Houses can't jump.

## 🦖 DINO FACT

There are over 700 known extinct dinosaur species.

🦖 Fill the blank boxes by writing the number of the piece that fits in the square.

🦖 Remember that each picture should only appear once in each column, row, and small square.

**2**

**3**

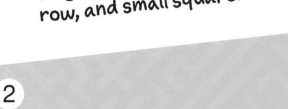

# Hooray!

Toppy's parents are free at last. Good work! Now to return the missing research and get out of here.

# THE FINAL PUSH

Having safely escaped from Dinosaur Island, the team runs back through the labs and makes it to the exit. There is just one more door to pass to get you back to the museum. The only problem is, it's locked. To complete your mission, you must figure out how to unlock it.

You're almost there. First, you need to look back through your notes.

- You'll need the five numbers that you jotted down.
- Then put these numbers into the triangle.
- Each side of the triangle must add up to nine. Good luck!

What numbers did you find? Write them here!

ATTEMPT 1

ATTEMPT 2

CHALLENGE
RATING

# Awesome job!

You're back in the museum with the capsule containing the *Giganotosaurus* fossils. Zane finds one of the resident paleontologists, who is delighted to receive a new exhibit for her museum. The team can't wait to tell Zinnia the good news.

# ANSWERS

## PAGES 10-11

## PAGES 12-13

1: **2**    2: **4**    3: **5**    4: **7**

## PAGES 14-15

| | | |
|---|---|---|
| 6 | 2 | 7 |
| 4 | 9 | 5 |
| 8 | 1 | 3 |

## PAGES 18-19

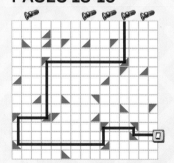

## PAGES 20-21

## PAGES 22-23

Door **8**
Door **4**
Door **3**
Door **2**
Door **5**
Door **7**
Door **1**
Door **6**

CODE: **8 3 2 6 1 4 7 5**

## PAGES 24-25

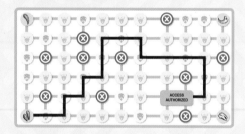

## PAGES 28-29

CODE: **5   2   7   8   4**

**Note 3 is the correct note.**

## PAGES 30-31

## PAGES 32-33

**8     15     7**

**PAGES 34-35**
1: **C**  2: **B**  3: **B**  4: **A**

**PAGES 36-37**
1: **A**  2: **D**  3: **F**  4: **H**  5: **E**  6: **C**

**PAGES 40-41**

**PAGES 42-43**

**PAGES 44-45**
**3 is the missing ripped piece of the poster.**

**PAGES 46-47**

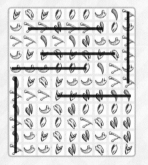

**PAGES 50-51**

**PAGES 52-53**

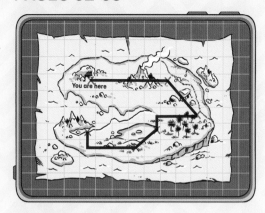

**PAGES 54-55**

 **5 is the correct capsule.**

**PAGES 56-57**
1: **C**  2: **A**  3: **H**

**PAGES 58-59**

1:   2:

3: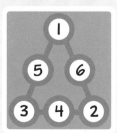

**PAGES 60-61**

# SEE YOU ON THE NEXT ADVENTURE!

Color in the team!